Arbor Day Book

History, Facts, Quizzes, Quotes

About Arbor Day

DEDICATION

Contents

What Is Arbor Day?

Arbor Day, much like Earth Day, is a holiday that celebrates nature.

Its purpose is to encourage people to plant trees, and many communities take the opportunity to organize tree-planting and litter-collecting events on or around the holiday.

A popular Arbor Day tradition is to plant a tree in honor or memory of a loved one.

Arbor Day sprouted from the mind of a zealous tree lover named Julius Sterling Morton, who had a passion for planting all kinds of trees. The first Arbor Day occurred on April 10, 1872, in Nebraska City, Nebraska.

When Is Arbor Day?

Today, Arbor Day is celebrated on the last Friday in April, although some states observe it on dates that better coincide with the local area's planting times. For instance, Hawaii celebrates Arbor Day on the first Friday of November, and Alaskans celebrate it on the third Monday in May.

The History of Arbor Day

- The first Arbor Day occurred on April 10, 1872, in Nebraska City, Nebraska. It's estimated that nearly one million trees were planted on this day.
- By April 22, 1885, Arbor Day had become a legal holiday in Nebraska. (The date was changed to April 22 to honor Morton's birthday, which was also the 22nd of April.)

- On that day, thousands of Nebraska City citizens turned out for one big party, including 1,000 school-children who formed a parade.
- Within 20 years of its creation, the holiday was celebrated in every American state except Delaware, which eventually joined in.
- Particularly pleasing to Morton was the fact that schools across the country began celebrating Arbor Day by dedicating the trees they planted to special people.
- Arbor Day was almost called Sylvan Day, which means "wooded." Several members of the Nebraska State Board of Agriculture favored it, but Morton argued that sylvan refers only to forest trees and that the name Arbor Day was most inclusive, covering forest trees and fruit trees.
- Today, the family home, Arbor Lodge, is a state park in Nebraska City, Nebraska.

- Over the years, Arbor Lodge grew from a four-room home into a 52-room mansion, complete with a terraced garden, a pine grove, and 65 acres of more than 250 varieties of trees and shrubs.
- J. Sterling Morton died at the age of 70 on April 27, 1902, writing just a month earlier that he hoped to plant trees as soon as the weather turned warm. A statue of him stands in the National Hall of Fame in Washington, D.C.

The Holiday Spreads

If you've ever seen a map of the Great Plains, you may have noticed that it's a bit larger than just the state of Nebraska. From the Mississippi to the Rockies, arid and semi-arid states in the Midwest and West started following Nebraska's example. They wanted to have more trees, too. By 1920, 45 states had adopted Arbor Day as a state holiday. The date of this holiday was changed from April 10 to April 22, J. Sterling Morton's birthday.

Today, all 50 states in the USA celebrate Arbor Day, as does Puerto Rico. The holiday now falls on the last Friday of April. While we still celebrate this day of trees, the ideology behind it has changed a little over time. Originally, Arbor Day was all about bringing the comforts of the East into the Great Plains, as well as expanding agriculture into this remote region. With agriculture firmly established throughout the West and Midwest, that was no longer the main priority behind the planting of trees by the 20th century.

Interesting Arbor Day Facts

• Laboratory research shows that trees are really good for us humans. Visual exposure to settings with trees has produced significant recovery from stress within five minutes, as indicated by changes in blood pressure and muscle tension.

• Trees are the largest living organism on Earth, with some coastal redwoods reaching over 360 feet tall and giant sequoias that can weigh 4 million pounds.

• Almost 98% of the weight of a tree is made up of six elements: carbon, hydrogen, oxygen, nitrogen, phosphorus and sulfur.

• They are also some of the oldest organisms on Earth. Some bristlecone pines are thought to be over 5000 years old.

• You probably remember from science class that trees produce oxygen, but you may not realize just how much. According to the U.S. Department of Agriculture (USDA), a single acre of forest absorbs six tons of carbon dioxide and puts out four tons of oxygen, which could meet the annual needs of 18 people.

• In addition to improved air quality, trees benefit water quality, too. Their roots in the ground mean less runoff and erosion, which in turn allows more recharging of the ground water supply. In addition, wooded areas help prevent the transport of sediment and chemicals into streams.

• There are over 23,000 different kinds of trees in the world.

• Trees are Mother Nature's air conditioners. The net cooling effect of a young, healthy tree is equivalent to 10 room-size air conditioners operating 20 hours a day. In fact, the USDA says that you can save 20 to 40 percent in energy used for heating with properly placed trees around buildings.

• Tree roots do not grow very deep and most tree roots are in the top 12 inches of soil, but they are wide. Tree roots often extend two to three times the width of the tree.

• Arbor Day didn't start small. On the first Arbor Day in 1872, an estimated one million trees were planted in Nebraska.

• Arbor means tree in Latin.

• The date that a country celebrates its own Arbor Day can vary, depending on the planting season and climate.

- Birdsey Northrop was chairman of the committee to introduce Arbor Day around the world. He was the first to introduce it to Japan and introduce the Japanese to Arbor Day in 1883.

- On April 22, 1885 Arbor Day became a legal holiday in Nebraska, the state where it originated. 1000 children formed a parade on that day.

- 20 years later, every state in America celebrated Arbor Day, aside from Delaware. Delaware eventually joined the Arbor Day celebrations.

- Arbor Day was almost named Sylvan Day. Arbor Day was chosen because arbor represented forest and fruit trees while sylvan only represented forest trees.

- J. Sterling Morton, who founded Arbor Day, built a family home that looked like the White House. Today the home and its 65 acres are known as Arbor Lodge and is now a state park. It is a 52 room mansion with over 250 different types of shrubs and trees.

- There is a statue of J. Sterling Morton in the National Hall of Fame in Washington D.C.

- J. Sterling Morton had the idea for Arbor Day because he thought there were not enough trees in Nebraska.

- Schools across the U.S. celebrate Arbor Day by having children plant a tree and dedicate it to someone special.

- In 1970, President Richard Nixon declared the last Friday in April to be Arbor Day.

- J. Sterling Morton's birthday was April 22nd. Arbor Day is usually celebrated on the last Friday in April in most states so that it ties in with Morton's birthday.

- Hawaii celebrates Arbor Day on the first Friday in November because of their planting season.

- Alaska celebrates Arbor Day on the third Monday in May.

- On the last Wednesday in September, Canada celebrates Maple Leaf Day, which falls during National Forest Week.

- In Ontario, Canada, they celebrate Arbor Week.

- The National Arbor Day Foundation held a vote for America's favorite tree in 2004. The mighty oak won by a landslide, earning 101,000 votes. America's National Tree is now the oak.

- One of the reasons that trees are so important is that they turn carbon dioxide into oxygen. They also provide shade, and grow fruit and nuts.

- Planting trees is not the only way to celebrate Arbor Day. Some people make donations to help save the rainforest. Some people help to educate others on the importance of trees. Participating in a recycling program is also another way to celebrate trees and the important role they play in our lives.

Arbor Day Quizzes

1. Which of the following building materials is renewable?

A. Cement

B. Steel

C. Wood

D. Brick

2. Which state was Arbor day first celebrated?

A. Oregon

B. Idaho

C. Nebraska

D. Minnesota

3. Paper bags were first measured by how many pounds (of which commodity) it would hold?

A. Sugar

B. Grain

C. Salt

D. Flour

4. What part of a tree transports food from the leaves to the rest of the tree?

A. Phloem

B. Crown

C. Branch

D. Bark

5. How many trees are planted in the U.S. each year?

A. 1.5 billion

B. >5 billion

C. 150 million

D. 1.5 million

6. True or False. Paper can be recycled forever?

A. False

B. True

7. Name a fruit that comes from a tree?

A. Mango

B. Pineapple

C. Strawberry

D. Watermelon

8. How do growing trees help combat global warming?

A. By absorbing in Nitrogen

B. By absorbing in Carbon Dioxide

C. By expelling Oxygen

D. By expelling Nitrogen

9. Name the term for trees that lose all their leaves or needles each year?

A. Tamarack

B. Deciduous

C. Pine

D. Coniferous

10. Who is the father of Arbor Day?

A. George Washington

B. Abraham Lincoln

C. J. Sterling Morton

D. Theodore Roosevelt

11. Why do we celebrate Arbor Day?

A. To advocate for a pollution-free world

B. To encourage people to plant and care for trees

C. To inspire awareness towards environmental issues

12. Arbor Day (USA) is observed on the last Friday of which month?

January

A. February

B. March

C. April

D. May

13. Which of these countries does NOT celebrate Arbor Day?

A. Brazil

B. China

C. Vietnam

D. India

E. The Philippines

14. In some countries, Arbor Day is also known as

A. National Tree Planting Day

B. Earth Day

C. Greenery Day

D. Tree Hugging Day

15. The term "arbor" means ______.

A. Greenery

B. Plant

C. Shrub

D. Tree

E. Forest

16. What is the most popular Arbor Day's activity?

A. Participate in a green concert

B. Recycle all household paper items

C. Plant new trees

D. Reduce energy usage

17. True or False. It was estimated that more than a million trees were planted in observance of the first American Arbor Day.

A. False

B. True

18. Which of these groups is the world's biggest tree-planting organization?

A. National Arbor Day Foundation

B. Sierra Club

C. Friends of the Earth

D. Wildlife Conservation Society

E. World Wide Fund for Nature

19. The first U.S. state to recognize Arbor Day was ______.

A. California

B. Kansas

C. New Hampshire

D. Iowa

E. Nebraska

20. True or False. Arbor Day is a federal holiday in the United States.

A. False

B. True

21. What year was the first Arbor Day celebrated?

A. 1872

B. 1932

C. 1962

22. What is the state tree of Michigan?

A. Sugar Maple

B. White Pine

C. Red Oak

23. What is the national tree?

A. Mighty Oak

B. Mighty Pine

C. Mighty Maple

24. Shade trees around your home can reduce your air conditioning needs by up to:

A. 30%

B. 50%

C. 70%

25. Cottonwood trees have seeds surrounded by white, fluffy hairs and can be carried in the wind for up to several:

A. Hours

B. Days

C. Weeks

26. How much land in the United States is covered by forest?

A. 10%

B. 30%

C. 50%

27. A single tree can produce enough oxygen each year for how many people?

A. 6

B. 4

C. 2

28. We need national forests because the average life of a tree in the city is only:

A. 8 years

B. 15 years

C. 20 years

Answer

1. C. Wood

Wood is the only raw building material that is increasing its reserves annually!

2. C. Nebraska

At a meeting of the Nebraska Board of Agriculture on January 4, 1872, Morton introduced a resolution that April 10th "be set apart and consecrated for tree planting in the State of Nebraska and that the State Board of Agriculture hereby name it Arbor Day." The resolution passed unanimously. Three months later, on April 10, 1872, the first-ever Arbor Day was celebrated in Nebraska.

3. A. Sugar

4. A. Phloem

Phloem, also called bast, tissues in plants that conduct foods made in the leaves to all other parts of the plant. Phloem is composed of various specialized cells called sieve tubes, companion cells, phloem fibres, and phloem parenchyma cells

5. A. 1.5 billion

1.5 billion seedlings are hand-planted annually in the U.S. in addition to what Nature plants.

6. A. False

False, the fibers that make up paper break down each time it is recycled and eventually are unable to be used to make recycled paper.

7. A. Mango

Mango, Mangifera indica, is an evergreen tree in the family Anacardiaceae grown for its edible fruit. The mango tree is erect and branching with a thick trunk and broad, rounded canopy. The leaves of the tree are are shiny and dark green.

8. B. By absorbing in Carbon Dioxide

Growing trees take in carbon dioxide, a greenhouse gas!

9. B. Deciduous

Deciduous means "falling off at maturity" or "tending to fall off", and it is typically used in order to refer to trees or shrubs that lose their leaves seasonally (most commonly during autumn) and to the shedding of other plant structures such as petals after flowering or fruit when ripe.

10. C. J. Sterling Morton

Julius Sterling Morton - a successful newspaper editor, politician, avid conservationist, and Secretary of Agriculture - is most revered as the man who first proposed the idea of Arbor Day, a world-wide holiday devoted to tree planting and care. Arbor Day is the last Friday In April (April 28. 2017)

11. B. To encourage people to plant and care for trees

12. D. May

13. C. Vietnam

14. A. National Tree Planting Day

15. D. Forest

16. C. Plant new trees

17. B. True

18. A. National Arbor Day Foundation

19. E. Nebraska

20. A. False

21. A. 1872

22. B. White Pine

23. A. Mighty Oak

24. A. 30%

25. B. Days

26. B. 30%

27. C. 2

28. 8 years

Arbor Day Quotes

- "The wonder is that we can see these trees and not wonder more." -- Ralph Waldo Emerson

- "If a man walks in the woods for love of them half of each day, he is in danger of being regarded as a loafer. But if he spends his days as a speculator, shearing off those woods and making the earth bald before her time, he is deemed an industrious and enterprising citizen." -- Henry David Thoreau

- "He who plants a tree plants a hope." -- Lucy Larcom

- "Even if I knew that tomorrow the world would go to pieces, I would still plant my apple tree." -- Martin Luther

- “The clearest way into the Universe is through a forest wilderness.” — John Muir

- “The creation of a thousand forests is in one acorn.” — Ralph Waldo Emerson

- “Love the trees until their leaves fall off, then encourage them to try again next year.” — Chad Sugg

- “A nation that destroys its soils destroys itself. Forests are the lungs of our land, purifying the air and giving fresh strength to our people. ” — Franklin D. Roosevelt

- “To be poor and be without trees, is to be the most starved human being in the world. To be poor and have trees, is to be completely rich in ways that money can never buy." — Clarissa Pinkola Estés, The Faithful Gardener: A Wise Tale About That Which Can Never Die

- "Trees are poems that the earth writes upon the sky." — Kahlil Gibran, Sand and Foam

- "When trees burn, they leave the smell of heartbreak in the air." —Jodi Thomas, Welcome to Harmony

- "All our wisdom is stored in the trees." — Santosh Kalwar

- "Fancy cutting down all those beautiful trees…to make pulp for those bloody newspapers, and calling it civilisation." —Winston Churchill, remarking to his son during a visit to Canada in 1929

- "The planting of a tree, especially one of the long-living hardwood trees, is a gift which you can make to posterity at almost no cost and with almost no trouble, and if the tree takes root it will far outlive the visible effect of any of your other actions, good or evil." — George Orwell

- "To the great tree-loving fraternity we belong. We love trees with universal and unfeigned love, and all things that do grow under them or around them – the whole leaf and root tribe." — Henry Ward Beecher

- "In a forest of a hundred thousand trees, no two leaves are alike. And no two journeys along the same path are alike." —Paulo Coelho, Aleph

- "In nature, nothing is perfect and everything is perfect. Trees can be contorted, bent in weird ways, and they're still beautiful." — Alice Walker

- "I thank you god for this most amazing day, for the leaping greenly spirits of trees, and for the blue dream of sky and for everything which is natural, which is infinite, which is yes." — E. E. Cummings

- "Trees are the earth's endless effort to speak to the listening heaven." — Rabindranath Tagore

- "If you cut down a forest, it doesn't matter how many sawmills you have if there are no more trees." — Susan George

- "Hugging trees has a calming effect on me. I'm talking about enormous trees that will be there when we are all dead and gone. I've hugged trees in every part of this little island." — Gerry Adams

- "The more often we see the things around us — even the beautiful and wonderful things — the more they become invisible to us. That is why we often take for granted the beauty of this world: the flowers, the trees, the birds, the clouds — even those we love. Because we see things so often, we see them less and less." — Joseph B. Wirthlin

- "Trees love to toss and sway; they make such happy noises." — Emily Carr

- "He plants trees to benefit another generation." — Caecilius Statius

- "Knowing trees, I understand the meaning of patience. Knowing grass, I can appreciate persistence." — Hal Borland

- "I plant a lot of trees. I am a great believer in planting things for future generations. I loathe the now culture where you just live for today." — Penelope Keith

- "Trees go wandering forth in all directions with every wind, going and coming like ourselves, traveling with us around the sun two million miles a day, and through space heaven knows how fast and far!" — John Muir

- "I am going to try to pay attention to the spring. I am going to look around at all the flowers, and look up at the hectic trees. I am going to close my eyes and listen." — Anne Lamott

- "The creation of a thousand forests is in one acorn." -- Ralph Waldo Emerson

- "The clearest way into the universe is through a forest wilderness." — John Muir
- "Acts of creation are ordinarily reserved for gods and poets. To plant a pine, one need only own a shovel." — Aldo Leopold
- "I never before knew the full value of trees. Under them I breakfast, dine, write, read and receive my company." — Thomas Jefferson
- "He that plants trees loves others beside himself." — Thomas Fuller
- "Those who contemplate the beauty of the earth find reserves of strength that will endure as long as life lasts. There is something infinitely healing in the repeated refrains of nature—the assurance

that dawn comes after night, and spring after the winter." — Rachel Carson

- "The time is always ripe to do right." — Martin Luther King, Jr.
- "The best friend on earth of man is the tree. When we use the tree respectfully and economically, we have one of the greatest resources on earth." — Frank Lloyd Wright
- "I am myself and what is around me, and if I do not save it, it shall not save me." — Jose Ortega Y Gasset
- "He who plants a tree plants a hope." — Lucy Larcom
- Holy Mother Earth, the trees and all nature are witnesses of your thoughts and deeds." — Winnebago Saying
- "The earth brought forth vegetation, plants yielding seed according to their own kinds, and trees bearing fruit in which is their

seed, each according to its kind. And God saw that it was good." — Genesis 1:12

- "To exist as a nation, to prosper as a state, and to live as a people, we must have trees." — Theodore Roosevelt
- "Never doubt that a small group of thoughtful, committed citizens can change the world. Indeed, it's the only thing that ever has." — Margaret Mead
- "A people without children would face a hopeless future: a country without trees is almost as hopeless; forests which are so used that they cannot renew themselves will soon vanish, and with them, all their benefits." — Theodore Roosevelt
- "I am the heat of your hearth, the shade screening you from the sun; I am the beam that holds your house, the board of your table; I am the handle of your hoe, the door of your homestead, the wood of

your cradle, and the shell of your coffin. I am the gift of God and the friend of man." — Unknown

- "The forests are the flags of Nature. They appeal to all and awaken inspiring universal feelings. Enter the forest and the boundaries of nations are forgotten. It may be that some time an immortal pine will be the flag of a united and peaceful world." — Enos A. Mills
- "In the woods we return to reason and faith." — Ralph Waldo Emerson
- "No shade tree? Blame not the sun but yourself." — Chinese Proverb
- "Trees are the Earth's endless effort to speak to the listening heaven." — Rabindranath Tagore
- "We make an immense mistake when we think of trees as solely an aesthetic member of a community. They cut pollution, they cool

the air, they prevent erosion, they muffle sound, they produce oxygen. Then, after all that, they look good." — Dr. Richard Leakey

- "I never saw a discontented tree. They grip the ground as though they liked it, and though fast rooted they travel about as far as we do. They go wandering forth in all directions with every wind, going and coming like ourselves, traveling with us around the sun two million miles a day, and through space heaven knows how fast and far!" – John Muir

- "The best time to plant a tree is twenty years ago. The second best time is now." – Chinese Proverb

- "Trees are sanctuaries. Whoever knows how to speak to them, whoever knows how to listen to them, can learn the truth. They do not preach learning and precepts, they preach undeterred by particulars, the ancient law of life." – Hermann Hesse, Wandering

- “What did the tree learn from the earth to be able to talk with the sky?” – Pablo Neruda

- “I am the Lorax! I speak for the trees, Which you seem to be chopping as fast as you please; But I also speak for the brown Barbaloots, Who frolicked and played in their Barbaloot suits, Happily eating Truffula fruits. Now, since you’ve chopped the trees to the ground There’s not enough Truffula fruit to go ’round! And my poor Barbaloots are all feeling the crummies Because they have gas, and no food, in their tummies.” – Dr. Seuss

- “The creation of a thousand forests is in one acorn.” – Ralph Waldo Emerson

- "Alone with myself
The trees bend to caress me
The shade hugs my heart" – Candy Polgar

- "Suburbia is where the developer bulldozes out the trees, then names the streets after them."- Bill Vaughan

- "Because they are primeval, because they outlive us, because they are fixed, trees seem to emanate a sense of permanence. And though rooted in earth, they seem to touch the sky. For these reasons it is natural to feel we might learn wisdom from them, to haunt about them with the idea that if we could only read their silent riddle rightly we should learn some secret vital to our own lives; or even, more specifically, some secret vital to our real, our lasting and spiritual existence." – Kim Taplin, Tongues in Trees

- "Someone's sitting in the shade today because someone planted a tree a long time ago."- Warren Buffett

- "The wonder is that we can see these trees and not wonder more."- Ralph Waldo Emerson

- "A society grows great when old men plant trees whose shade they know they shall never sit in."- Greek Proverb

- "It is well that you should celebrate your Arbor Day thoughtfully, for within your lifetime the nation's need of trees will become serious. We of an older generation can get along with what we have, though with growing hardship; but in your full manhood and womanhood you will want what nature once so bountifully supplied and man so thoughtlessly destroyed; and because of that want you will reproach us, not for what we have used, but for what we have wasted." – Theodore Roosevelt, 1907 Arbor Day Message

- "What we are doing to the forests of the world is but a mirror reflection of what we are doing to ourselves and to one another."- Mahatma Gandhi

- "Trees are poems that the earth writes upon the sky." – Kahlil Gibran

- "A tree is beautiful, but what's more, it has a right to life; like water, the sun and the stars, it is essential. Life on earth is inconceivable without trees." – Anton Chekhov

- As the poet said, "only God can make a tree" — probably because it's so hard to figure out how to get the bark on. – Woody Allen

Arbor Day: Messages, Wishes & Greetings

- Plant a tree and see the Mother earth thanking you with a smile.

- It is time to think seriously about the survival of the earth.

- God created the earth with lots of trees and other natural things. We destroyed it. Now its time to recycle.

- Plant more trees and make the earth beautiful and a perfect place to live.

- Celebrate this Arbor Day in the shade of your own trees.

- Make a tree as your friend and you will not regret!

- God loves us which is why created this beautiful earth and gave to mankind.

- Before cutting a tree, just remember that we too are creatures on earth and one day should leave this world. Do good to earth before you leave.

- Show your gratitude to earth by planting trees.

- Oxygen is necessary for our living but even knowing that we cut trees. A tragedy!

- We cannot find peace under a building but under a tree.

- There is music on the earth when trees blow air.

- Present your future generation with beautiful earth. Plat a tree now.

- The earth really looks beautiful now with all greenery because our forefathers have planted a tree in their time.

- Plant hope for a better future by plating a tree.

- It is your duty to do what you can for the earth.

- Invest wisely with green and the fruit is countless!

- To write a poem everyone needs a natural place to think about it and we need to do something to preserve nature to get such lovely poems.

- Before it's too late, let's plant a tree.
- The importance of a tree is realized when we struggle to breathe!
- Keep your earth on style by making it green.
- On Arbor day, gift a plant to your friends and dear ones to create awareness.
- Celebrate this day under a tree not on the Internet!
- Don't judge others for destroying the planet, plant a tree!
- Let's not create a history of forests and greenery. But let's educate everyone to make history by planting trees.

- Do an act of kindness no matter how small is that. Saplings are always small but when it becomes a tree, it bears fruits!

- Give thanks to mother nature by planting trees.

- All the creatures on earth are depended on each other. Our mother earth depends on us! Save the earth!

- Arbor Day is not like other holidays, it might not have the enjoyment of partying, but the enjoyment of planting a tree.

- Be generous towards the earth. One day it will also be generous to you!

-

- Let's vow today to protect our mother nature. Happy Arbor Day.

- Let's keep our earth fresh for our future generation. Let us preserve the fresh air which we are enjoying now.

- I strongly believe in God and my God is nature.

- Plan a good harvest and plant a tree.

- We sit under the shade of a tree today since someone has planted that tree a long time ago.

- Make life by giving. Give something good to nature today and it will be thankful to you till the end.

- You are always responsible for your deeds.

- Let's show our humanity on trees to save them and to save ourselves.

- We never saw heaven. Let's create that heaven on earth if not whole, but a piece of it!

- There should be a law like no food if no trees planted.

- Love nature and it will love you!

- Today is Arbor Day. Plant a tree, no regrets.

- Give surprise to your eyes, by seeing greenery everywhere.

- Recycle the things you can and save our earth!

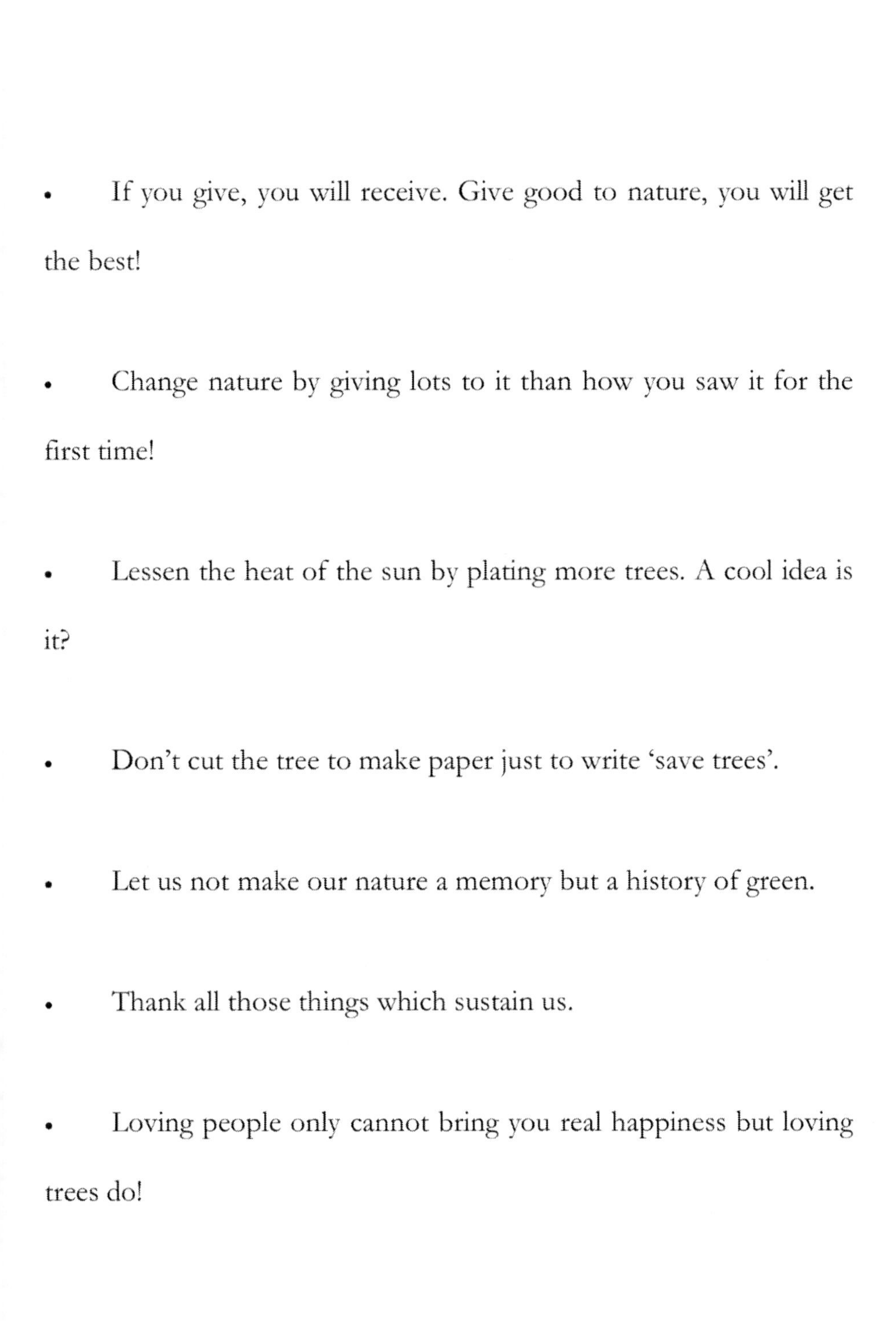

- If you give, you will receive. Give good to nature, you will get the best!

- Change nature by giving lots to it than how you saw it for the first time!

- Lessen the heat of the sun by plating more trees. A cool idea is it?

- Don't cut the tree to make paper just to write 'save trees'.

- Let us not make our nature a memory but a history of green.

- Thank all those things which sustain us.

- Loving people only cannot bring you real happiness but loving trees do!

- Spread the love of nature everywhere you go by planting trees.

- Feel the nature and you will not regret.

- Earth is the mother of all people and the people have a responsibility towards her.

- Today is Arbor Day and if you haven't started yet, let us do the new beginning!

- Witness a thousand miracles by walking in nature.

- Nature is not meant for the picnic but it is your home!

- Let us take an oath to make our surroundings greener and happier by planting trees, watering them and taking care of them with our heart and soul…. Sending best wishes to you on National Arbor Day with a hope that you will join the wagon!!!

- Trees are an essential part of our lives….. And today is the day to promise ourselves to have them in greater numbers and to make have liveliness and happiness around us…. With lots of love, wishing you a greener and blessed National Arbor Day.

- Planting a tree is like planting a hope….. It is the most beautiful present we all can give our coming generations…. So let's plant trees for a greener tomorrow…. Wishing you and your family a wonderful National Arbor Day.

- Each one, plant one…. With this thought, we can make our planet more beautiful, much greener and much healthier home…. Let us make an effort to plant trees on National Arbor Day and make it a memorable and meaningful day in every sense. Happy Arbor Day to you.

- By planting one tree, we are expressing our positive thought and hope.... Even if we are not there tomorrow, our trees will be there to take care of our generations to come..... Sending warm wishes to you on National Arbor Day my friend.

- For every country, its forest is like the lung to its land which gives fresh air to its countrymen.... Let us save our soil by planting trees..... Let us work to become a greener and happier nation.... Warm wishes to you on the amazing occasion of National Arbor Day.

- With a little effort today, we can make our future brighter..... By planting one tree today, we can aim to create a healthier tomorrow for our coming generations…. Let us celebrate National Arbor Day by promising to plant one tree every year!!!

- Let us leave something precious behind us, something productive, something that will make us remember for our good karmas….. Let us plant trees and take care of them as a present for our young ones….. Wishing you a very Happy Arbor Day my dear.

- They look beautiful standing tall in peace….. They infuse harmony as they stand wise in silence…. They give us air, they give us shed, they give us flowers, they give us fruits…. We surely don't need more reasons to plant trees….. Happy National Arbor Day.

- Planting a tree is our responsibility to save our Earth and to make it a greener place to live…. Let us fulfill this onus by planting trees on National Arbor Day with love and care…. To plant a new hope, to plant a new life….. Warm wishes on National Arbor Day to you.

- Trees are like beautiful poems written on sky by earth. Let us not destroy these life giving creations as they are precious gifts of nature. Wishing you a National Arbor Day 2020.

- Let us not reach to a point when all trees have cut down for our needs and we have nothing to eat or drink or breathe. Let us conserve them by joining hands. Happy National Arbor Day to you.

- Trees are like blessings of Earth on mankind. They give us flowers, fruits, shelter, air and love to life a happy and healthy life. Let us plant more trees and save them. Happy National Arbor Day.

- The real meaning of life lies in planting trees and saving the ones our ancestors have planted. Let us promise ourselves to plant more and more trees. Best wishes on National Arbor Day to you.

- Sitting under a tree on a hot summer day is the love of the tree in form of shadow. Let us return the innumerable favors of trees by conserving them. Warm wishes on National Arbor Day 2020.

- On the occasion of National Arbor Day, let us join hands to save trees and plant more and more trees this year for a healthier and greener planet. Wishing Happy National Arbor Day to you.

- Let us leave a healthier planet Earth for our children by planting more and more trees today. Let us bring more positivity and greenery by saving and protecting trees. Happy National Arbor Day.

- We don't need a day to save a tree. We don't need a date to plan a tree. We don't need a reason to save our planet. It is our responsibility. Wishing Happy National Arbor Day to you and your family.

- Tall standing trees always inspire us to plant more and more trees to save our planet. Let us plant one tree per person for a greener planet. Happy National Arbor Day 2020 to you.

- To the trees which have always been giving, let us come together to water them, save them and multiply them by planting more trees. Best wishes on National Arbor Day to you and your family.